Measures

to level 3

Paul Harrison

Hodder & Stoughton
A MEMBER OF THE HODDER HEADLINE GROUP

The author and publishers are grateful for the comments and advice received from staff and pupils at schools involved in the trialling of materials for this series:

Bedminster Down School, Bristol
Rainham School for Girls, Kent
Archers Court School, Kent
Mark Hall School, Essex
The Gillingham College, Kent
Churchill Community School, North Somerset
St Martin's School, Derbyshire
Woodlands School, Essex
Brigshaw High School, Leeds
Portway Community School, Bristol
Aldercar School, Derbyshire

The author wishes to give special thanks to Mike Ward of Roade School, Northamptonshire for his helpful comments and suggestions.

The cover illustration for this series is by Sarah Jones.

Orders; please contact Bookpoint Ltd, 39 Milton Park, Abingdon, Oxon OX14 4TD. Telephone: (44) 01235 400414, Fax: (44) 01235 400454. Lines are open from 9.00–6.00, Monday to Saturday, with a 24 hour message answering service.
Email address: orders@bookpoint.co.uk

British Library Cataloguing in Publication Data
A catalogue record for this title is available from the British Library

ISBN 0 340 74910 5

First published 1999
Impression number   10 9 8 7 6 5 4 3 2 1
Year   2005 2004 2003 2002 2001 2000 1999

Copyright © 1999 Paul Harrison

All rights reserved. No part of this publication may be reproduced or transmitted in any form or by any means, electronic or mechanical, including photocopying, recording or any information storage and retrieval system, without permission in writing from the publisher or under licence from the Copyright Licensing Agency Limited. Further details of such licences (for reprographic reproduction) may be obtained from the Copyright Licensing Agency Limited, of 90 Tottenham Court Road, London W1P 9HE.

Typeset by GreenGate Publishing Services, Tonbridge, Kent.
Printed in Great Britain for Hodder and Stoughton Educational, a division of Hodder Headline Plc, 338 Euston Road, London NW1 3BH, by Hobbs the Printers, Totton, Hampshire.

Contents

Length Unit 1
    Measuring in metres   4
    Measuring in centimetres   5

Weight Unit 1
    Introducing the kilogram   6
    Weighing to the nearest kilogram   7

Capacity Unit 1
    Introducing the litre   8
    Using millilitres   9

Time Unit 1
    'Minutes past' times   10
    'Minutes past' and 'minutes to' times   11

Length Unit 2
    Metres and centimetres   12
    Choosing equipment and units   13

Weight Unit 2
    Weighing to the nearest 100 grams   14
    Using kitchen scales   15

Capacity Unit 2
    Choosing units and estimates   16
    Capacity problems   17

Time Unit 2
    Calculating with time   18
    Timetable problems   19

Length Unit 3
    Introducing the kilometre   20
    Choosing units and estimates   21

Weight Unit 3
    Personal weights   22
    Estimating weights   23

Glossary of buzzwords   24

LENGTH UNIT 1
Measuring in metres

On this page you will learn how to estimate and measure in metres

BUZZWORD

Estimate means **make a careful guess**.

You will need a metre stick or tape.

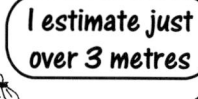

I estimate about 4 metres

I estimate just over 3 metres

Kody and Suzie measure the length of their go-kart. Kody uses a metre stick. Suzie uses a metre tape.

They find out that the go-kart is just under 3 metres long.

Estimate, then measure these in metres.

❶ A cupboard

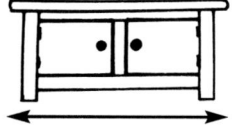

❷ A bench

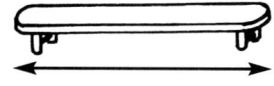

❸ A display board

❹ A door

Words you could use: about, just under, roughly, just over, nearly, almost, half

❺ The length of a wall

❻ The length of a bookshelf

For 3 **metres** we can write 3 **m**. Rewrite these using **m**:

❼ 6 metres   ❽ 5 metres   ❾ about 24 metres

CHALLENGE!

Place some things end to end until you think they measure about 1 metre. Check if you were right.

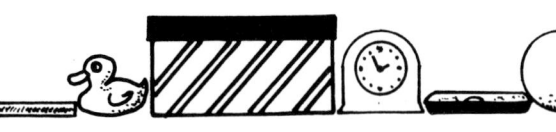

LENGTH UNIT 1

Measuring in centimetres

On this page you will learn how to estimate and measure in centimetres

BUZZWORD

Do you remember what **estimate** means? (page 4)

You will need a ruler with centimetres.

Metres are too big for measuring some things so we use **centimetres**.
1 metre = 100 centimetres.   This is 1 centimetre ├──┤

We can use a ruler for measuring centimetres.

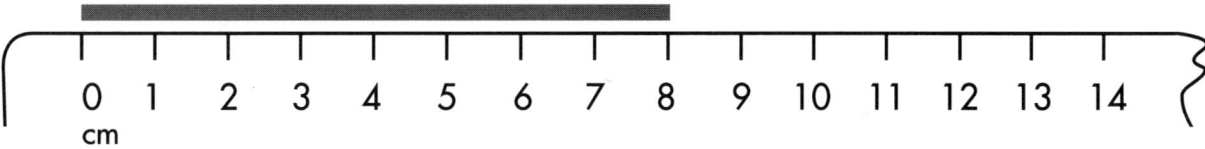

The thick line is **8 centimetres** or **8 cm** long.

Estimate and then measure how long these lines are. Use **cm**.

❶ ├──────────────┤

❷ ├─────────────────────────────────┤

❸ ├────────────────────┤

❹ ├──────────────────────────────────────┤

❺ ├──┤

Draw a line:

❻ 5 cm long.   ❼ 4 cm long.   ❽ 3 cm long.   ❾ 12 cm long.

Estimate and measure these in centimetres:

❿ Your handspan.   ⓫ Your first finger.

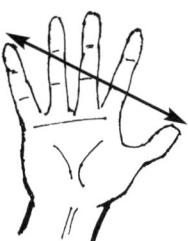   

Livewire: Measures to level 3

Introducing the kilogram

On this page you will learn how to find out whether things weigh more than less than, or about the same as one kilogram

BUZZWORDS

Approximately means **about the same as**.
Do you remember what **estimate** means? (page 4)

You will need a balance, two kilogram weights and things to weigh.

Shaun uses a balance and a kilogram weight.

He finds out that one of his rollerblades weighs less than one kilogram (1 kg).

Say whether these things weigh **more than**, **less than** or **about the same as** one kilogram.

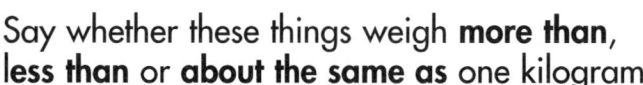

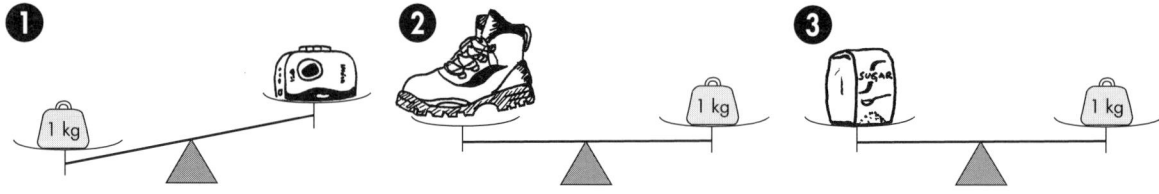

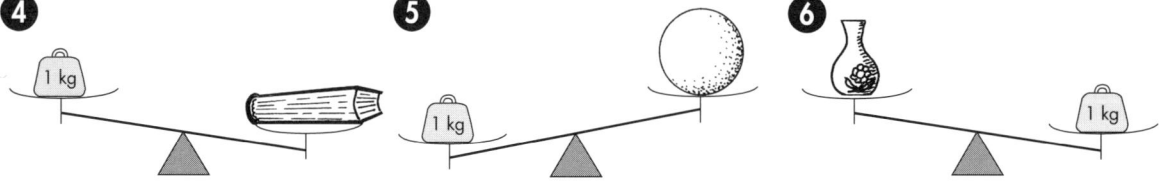

❼ Choose five objects that you **estimate** each weigh more than 1 kg but less than 2 kg. Use a balance and two kilogram weights to check.

❽ Find 5 objects that weigh **approximately** 1 kg altogether. Write down what they are.

page 6

Livewire: Measures to level 3

Weighing to the nearest kilogram

On this page you will learn how to estimate and weigh to the nearest kilogram using kitchen scales

BUZZWORD

Do you remember what **approximately** means? (page 6)

You will need kitchen scales and objects to weigh.

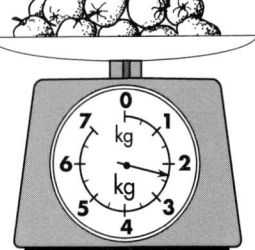

These apples weigh between 2 kg and 3 kg.
The pointer is nearer 2 kg than 3 kg.
We say the apples weigh 2 kg **to the nearest kilogram**.

What weights do these scales show to the nearest kilogram?

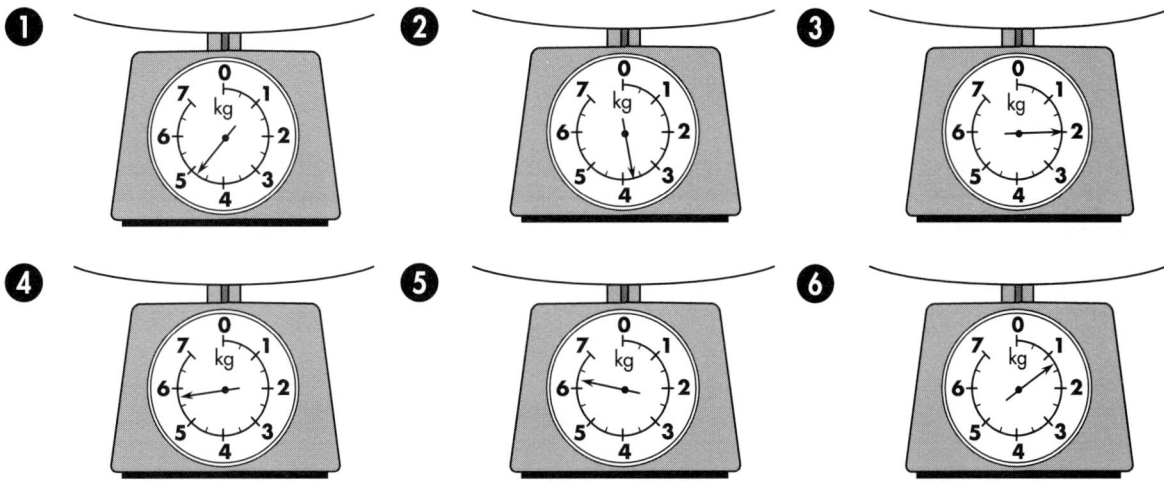

❼ Find 4 fairly heavy things that you can weigh with kitchen scales.
Record their weights to the nearest kilogram.

CHALLENGE!

Find 5 objects that you estimate will weigh **approximately** 2 kg altogether.
Weigh them. Was your estimate right?

Introducing the litre

On this page you will learn how to find out whether containers hold more than, about the same as or less than a litre

BUZZWORD

The **capacity** of something is how much it holds.
Do you remember what **estimate** means? (page 4)

You will need a collection of containers, a litre jug and water.

We can measure **capacity** in litres.
We can buy liquids like milk and cola in litre bottles.
We can use a litre jug to measure **capacity**.

Find some containers like these:

Look at a litre jug. Look at each container and **estimate** whether the **capacity** is:

more than 1 litre   less than 1 litre   or about 1 litre

Then fill the litre jug with water and check by pouring.

You could record your results like this or in another way.

container	estimate	check
large bowl	more than 1 litre	more than 1 litre

CHALLENGE!

- Find 5 things at home or in the supermarket that are sold in litre containers.
- Next time you are in a car filling up with fuel check how many litres it takes.

Using millilitres

On this page you will learn how to use millilitres to measure capacity

BUZZWORD

Do you remember what **capacity** means? (page 8) **Contains** means **has in it** or **holds**.

This **container** **contains** cola!

You will need a measuring jug or cylinder marked in 100 ml some small containers and water.

We use **millilitres** to measure capacities of less than 1 litre.

1 millilitre is about the size of a large raindrop.
The **capacity** of a teaspoon is about 5 millilitres.

1 litre = 1000 millilitres   1 l = 1000 ml

This measuring jug **contains** 700 ml of water.

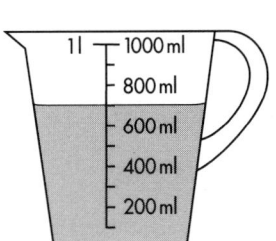

How many millilitres of water do these **contain**?

❶ 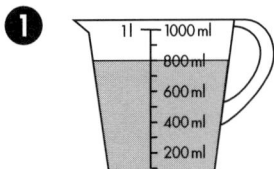 ❷ 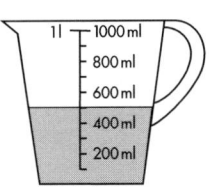 ❸ 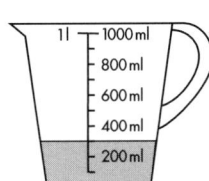 ❹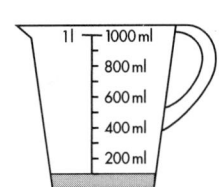

❺ Which jug **contains** half a litre?

❻ Find five containers like these that hold less than a litre.

Use water and a measuring jug to find the **capacity** of each container to the nearest 100 ml. Record your results.

Livewire: Measures to level 3

'Minutes past' times

On this page you will learn how to read and write the time in two ways, e.g: 8.35; 35 minutes past 8

2.40

40 minutes past 2

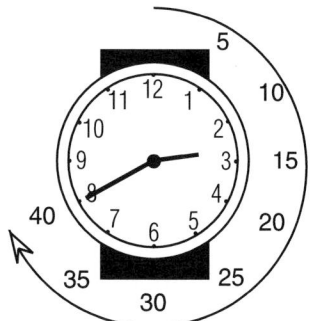

Write each time in two ways:

CHALLENGE!

Anna's alarm is going crazy!
It goes off every 25 minutes.

If it goes off at 2.00 o'clock what are the next 5 times it will go off?

'Minutes past' and 'minutes to' times

On this page you will learn how to read and write 'minutes to times'

> There are 60 **minutes** in an **hour**.

Times after 'half past' can be written in three ways:

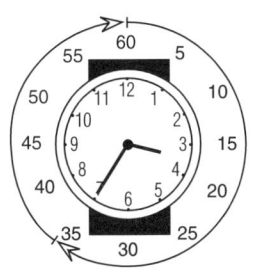

3.35

35 minutes past 3 or

25 minutes to 4

Write these times in three ways:

    ❷    ❸    ❹

❺    ❻    ❼    ❽

Write these as **minutes past** and **minutes to** times

❾    ❿    ⓫    ⓬

Livewire: Measures to level 3

LENGTH UNIT 2 — Metres and centimetres

On this page you will learn how to measure and record in metres and centimetres

BUZZWORDS

Length is how **long**.
Width is how **wide**.
Height is how **high** or **tall**.

You will need a metre stick or metre tape with centimetres.

Kylie is measuring the **height** of a shed.
It is 2 metres and 65 centimetres **high**.

She writes: **The wall is 2 m 65 cm high.**

Measure your classroom door in metres and centimetres.

What is its: ❶ **height**?   ❷ **width**?

Work with a friend. Measure each other's **height** in metres and centimetres.

❸ How **tall** is your friend?   ❹ How **tall** are you?   ❺ Who is **taller**?

❻ Find two things that are more than 1 metre **long**.
   Measure and write their **lengths** in metres and centimetres.

| Remember there are 100 centimetres in 1 metre. | 100 cm = 1 m. |
| 250 cm = 2 m 50 cm.   134 cm = 1 m 34 cm. | 305 cm = 3 m 5 cm. |

Change these lengths to m and cm.

❼ 325 cm   ❽ 410 cm   ❾ 405 cm   ❿ 65 cm

Change these lengths to cm:

⓫ 5 m 50 cm   ⓬ 3 m 25 cm   ⓭ 1 m 75 cm   ⓮ 0 m 50 cm

LENGTH UNIT 2

Choosing equipment and units

On this page you will learn how to choose the best equipment and most sensible estimates

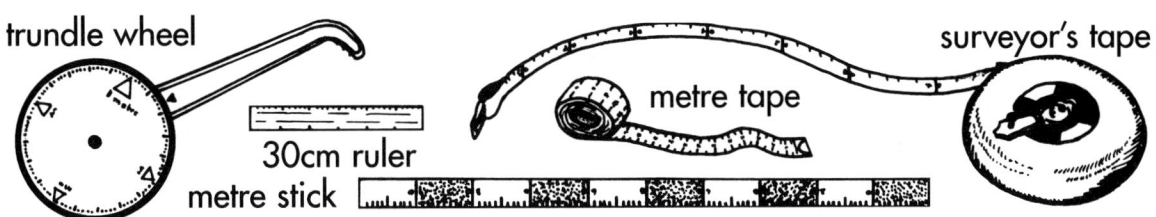

trundle wheel — 30cm ruler — metre stick — metre tape — surveyor's tape

To measure each thing below, decide and write down:

(a) what equipment you would use (choose from the picture above)

(b) what unit you would you use: metres or centimetres or both?

❶ A book

❷ Round a tree

❸ A curved path

❹ A carpet

❺ Round your wrist

❻ A pencil

Choose the most sensible estimate:

❼

about 2 m long
about 20 m long
about 20 cm long

❽

about 60 cm long
about 6 cm long
about 6 m long

❾

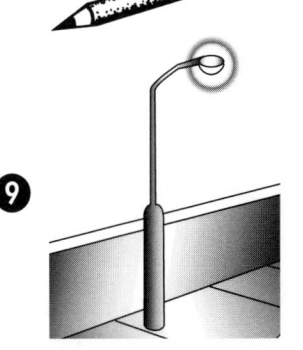

about 6 m high
about 60 cm high
about 60 m high

Livewire: Measures to level 3

Weighing to the nearest 100 grams

On this page you will learn how to weigh using kilograms and grams

BUZZWORDS

light	lighter	lightest	heavy	heavier	heaviest

You will need a balance and 1kg and 100 g weights.

We use **grams** for weighing things that are **lighter** than a kilogram.
1 kilogram = 1000 grams   1 kg = 1000 g

These weights balance the trainer.

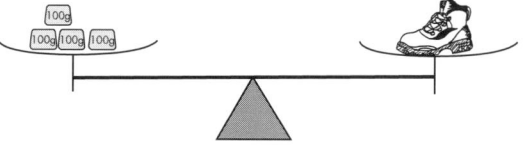

The shoe weighs about 400 grams.

These weights balance the book.

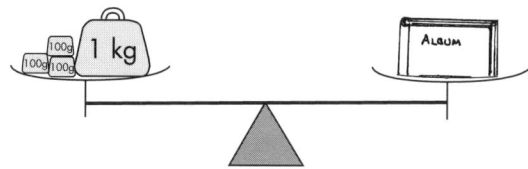

The book weighs about 1 kg 300 g.

❶ Use a balance and 1kg and 100 g weights.
Find three things **lighter** than a kilogram and three things **heavier** than a kilogram. Weigh each one and write the weight.

❷ Now write the weights in order from **lightest** to **heaviest**.

CHALLENGE!

Look for weights on labels at home or in the supermarket.
Find 5 that are **lighter** than 1 kilogram.
Find 3 that are **heavier** than 1 kilogram.
Write down what they are and their weights.

WEIGHT UNIT 2 — Using kitchen scales

On this page you will learn how to weigh to the nearest 100 grams using kitchen scales

You will need kitchen scales and things to weigh.

Each small division on these kitchen scales is 100 grams
They show 2 kg 600 g to the nearest 100 g

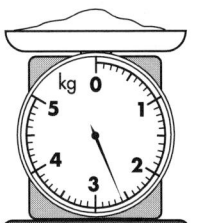

1 What weights do these scales show to the nearest 100 g?

A) 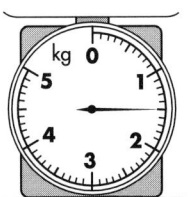   B)    C)

D) 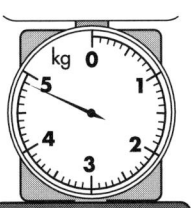   E) 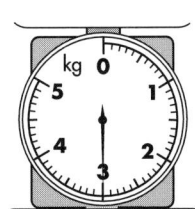   F)

Which scales show the **heavier** weight:

2 A or B?

3 B or C?

Which scales show the **lighter** weight:

4 C or D?

5 E or F?

Which scales show:

6 the **heaviest** weight of all?   **7** the **lightest** weight of all?

8 Use kitchen scales to weight 6 things to the nearest 100 g.

Write down the weights in order from lightest to heaviest.

Livewire: Measures to level 3

CAPACITY UNIT 2
Choosing units and estimates

Here you will learn how to choose units for measuring capacities and choose the most sensible estimates

BUZZWORD

Do you remember what **capacity** means? (page 8)

Which is the best unit for measuring the **capacity** of these – litres or millilitres?

1 a bath    **2** an egg cup    **3** a swimming pool

4 a glass    **5** a bucket    **6** a soup bowl

Choose the most sensible estimate:

7

5 ml   500 ml   5 l

8

10 ml   1 l   50 ml

9

1 l   20 l   200 l

10

200 l   200 ml

11

500 ml   50 ml   5 l

12

200 ml   2 l   20 ml

page 16   Livewire: Measures to level 3

Capacity problems

On this page you will solve problems about capacity

Zak starts a cycle race with 500 ml of drink in his bottle. Work out how much he has drunk from each of these bottles.

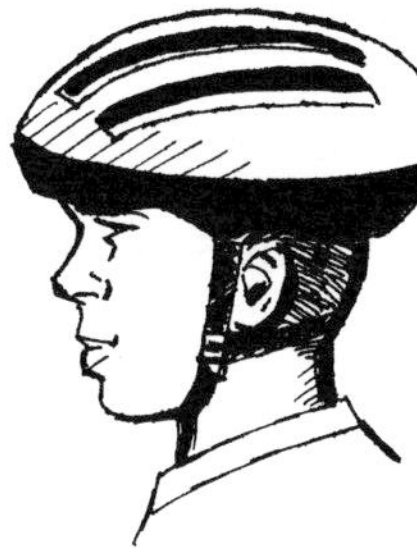

1 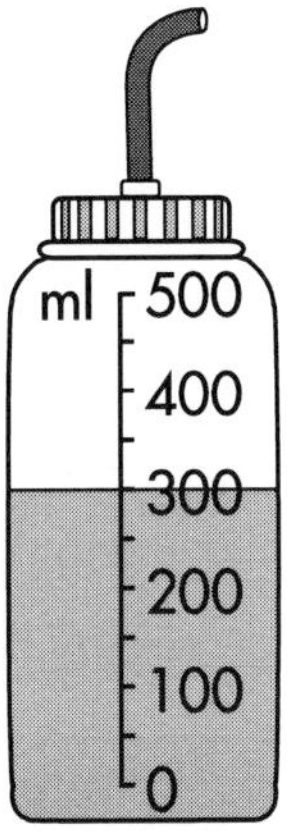 **2** 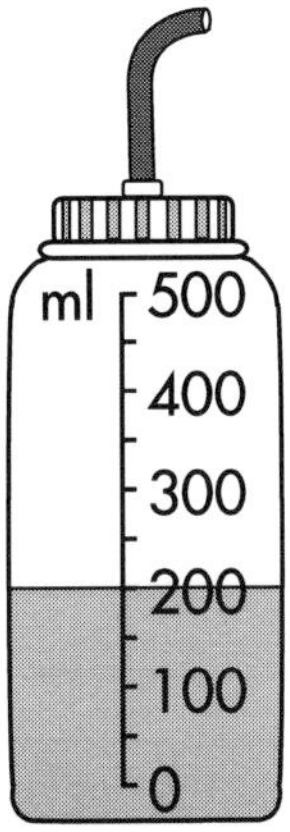 **3** 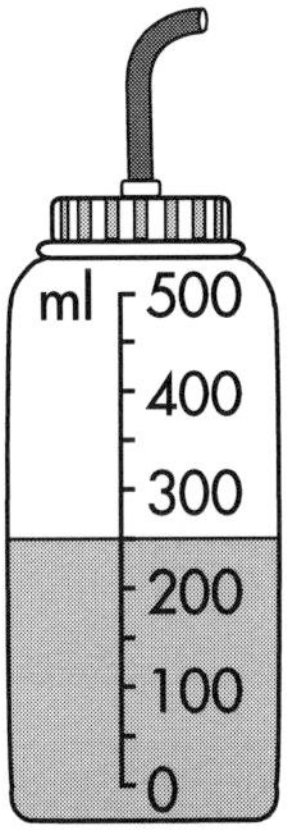 **4**

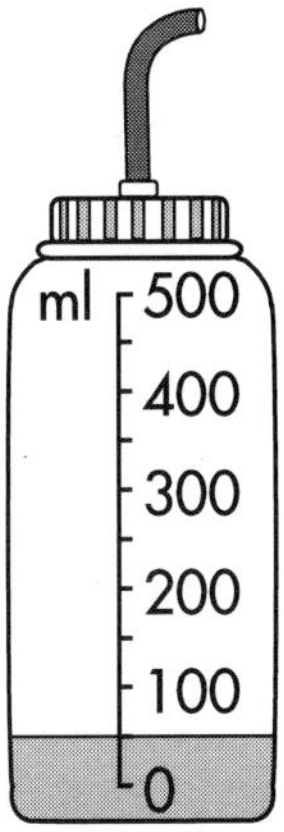

How many millilitres will be taken each day?

5 Hair Curler
Take four
5 ml spoonfuls
a day

6 Increase your
BRAINPOWER!
Take two
5 ml spoonfuls
twice a day

7 NIGHTSIGHT
for seeing in the dark
Take three
5 ml spoonfuls
three times
a day

If the bottles each contain 200 ml, how many days will each bottle last?

Livewire: Measures to level 3

Calculating with time

On this page you will learn how to work out how long it is between two times

Do you remember how many **minutes** there are in an **hour**? (page 11)

To work out how long things take it helps to count in fives.

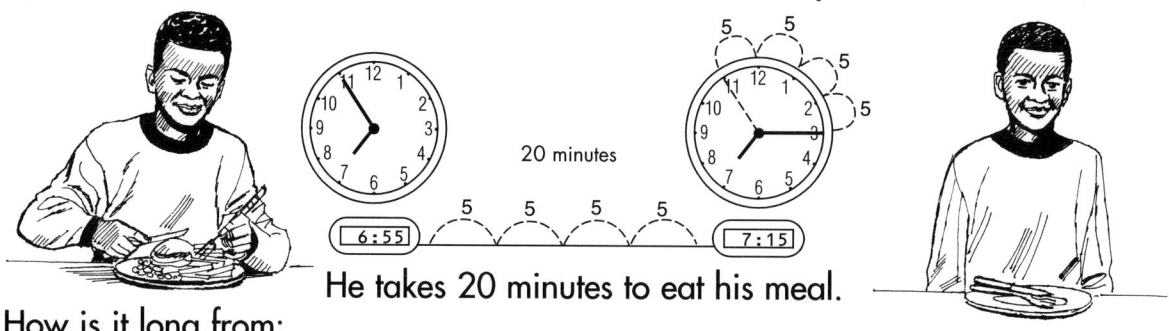

He takes 20 minutes to eat his meal.

How is it long from:

❸ 4:30 to 5:05   ❹ 1:15 to 1:55

❺ 2.35 to 2.45   ❻ 5.15 to 5.50   ❼ 12.15 to 1.05   ❽ 1.25 to 2.00

From 6.30 to 8.45 is longer than an hour. We need to count in hours first

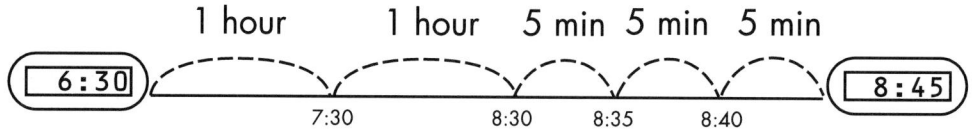

2 hours 15 minutes

How long is it from:

❾ 6.30 to 7.50?   ❿ 5.40 to 6.50?

⓫ 7.30 to 10.45?   ⓬ 2.45 to 5.50?

You could draw a time line to help you

Timetable Problems

On this page you will learn how to calculate times from a TV programme timetable

BUZZWORDS

Is longer means takes more time. **Is shorter** means takes less time.

Supersatellite TV Evening Programmes		Digitelly Evening Programmes	
6.00	S S News	6.00	Film: Masked Invaders
6.25	Comedy Time	7.35	Pop Quiz
7.10	Sports Review	8.15	Micky the Mouth Chat Show
7.50	Film: California Kid	9.00	D T News
10.00	The Billy Boxer Show	9.35	Film: The Lost Prince
10.55	Snooker Championships	11.10	Match of the day
12.15	Close	12.30	Close

How long do each of these Supersatellite programmes last?

❶ News   ❷ Film: California Kid   ❸ Snooker Championships

How long do each of these Digitelly programmes last?

❹ Pop Quiz   ❺ Film: The Lost Prince   ❻ Match of the Day

❼ How long is it between the end of Sports Review and the start of The Lost Prince?

❽ Which programme **is longer**: The Billy Boxer Show or Micky the Mouth Chat Show? How much **longer**?

❾ Which programme **is shorter**: S S News or D T News? How much **shorter**?

CHALLENGE!

You have a blank 2 hour video cassette. Which three programmes could you record? Give three different answers.

LENGTH UNIT 3 — Introducing the kilometres

On this page you will learn about kilometres and how to use a map to solve problems about distance

BUZZWORD

Distance is another word for **length**. **Via** means **going through**.

Long **distances** are sometimes measured in kilometres (km).
1 kilometre = 1000 metres   1 km = 1000 m

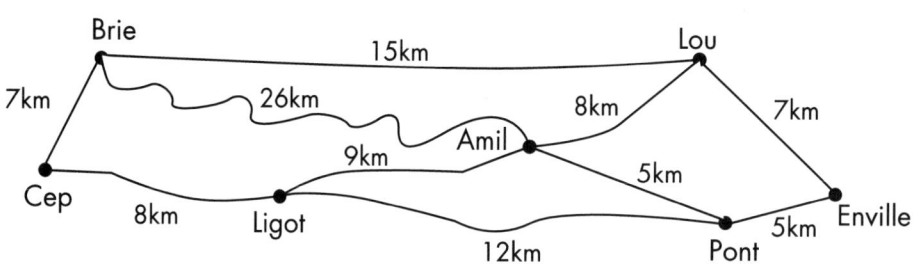

The shortest **distance** by road from Cep to Lou is 7 km + 15 km = 22 km
What is shortest **distance** by road from:

❶ Cep to Pont?   ❷ Pont to Lou?

❸ Ligot to Lou?   ❹ Amil to Cep?

How far is it from Enville to Brie: ❺ **via** Lou?   ❻ **via** Pont and Amil?

❼ Which is the longer journey:
   a) from Brie to Lou or
   b) from Brie to Amil?

   How much longer?

❽ Which is the shorter journey from Amil to Enville:
   a) **via** Lou or
   b) **via** Pont?

   How much shorter?

CHALLENGE!

You start at Brie. You want to visit all the villages in one journey. You do not want to go through any village twice. How could you do this in the shortest **distance**?

Write the villages you visit in order. What is the total **distance**?

LENGTH UNIT 3
Choosing units and estimates

On this page you will learn how to choose the best units to measure with

Which would be best for measuring these – centimetres, metres or kilometres?

1

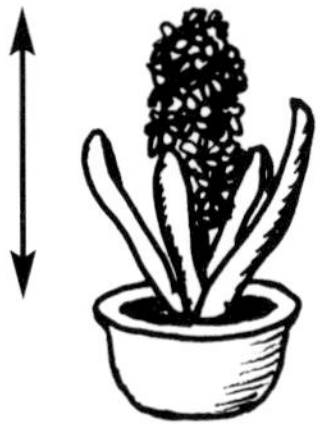

2

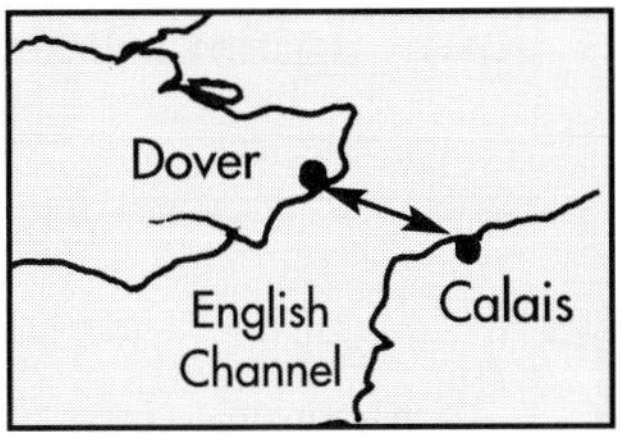

3

4 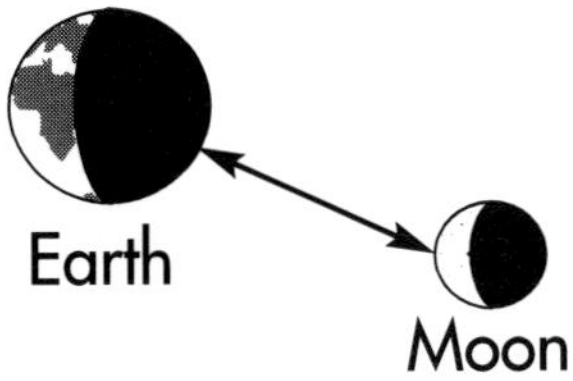 Earth — Moon

5

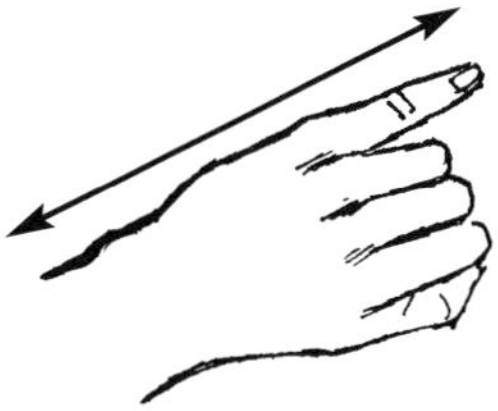

6

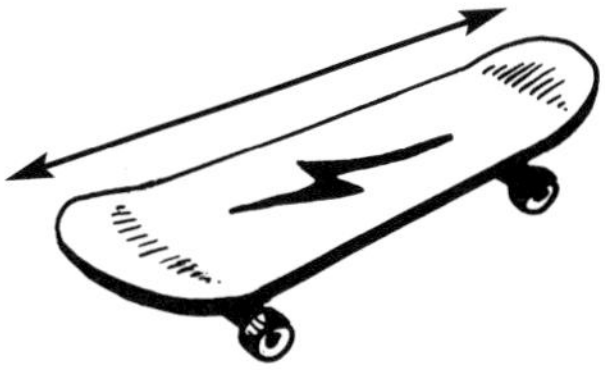

7

8  height

9 waist

Put the correct unit in each sentence: centimetres, metres or kilometres.

10 The length of the River Thames is 346 _____.

11 One of the longest snakes in the world is the Anaconda. It can be as long as 10 _____ .

12 The Severn rail tunnel is the longest tunnel in Britain. It is just over 7 _____ long.

13 An adult harvest mouse is about 6 _____ long.

Livewire: Measures to level 3

page 21

Personal weights

On this page you will learn how to use personal or bathroom scales

BUZZWORDS

Do you remember these words?
heavy, **heavier**, **heaviest**; **light**, **lighter**, **lightest** (page 14).

You will need personal or bathroom scales

William weighs 46 kg.

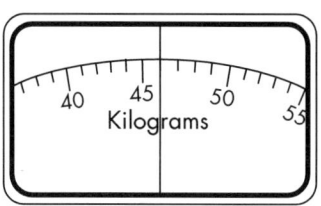

What do these people weigh?

1 Lucy   **2** Shona   **3** Liam   **4** Hanif

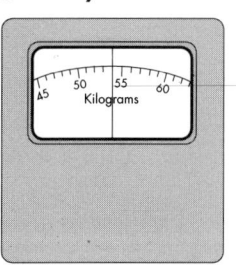 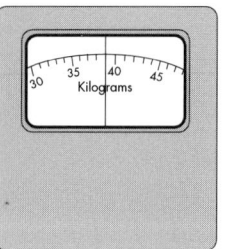 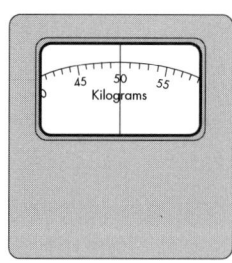 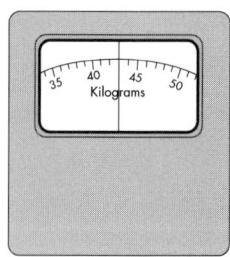

5 Who is **heaviest**?   **6** Who is **lightest**?

7 How much **heavier** than Shona is Liam?

8 How much **lighter** than Lucy is Hanif?

9 How **heavy** are Lucy and Shona together?

CHALLENGE!

Work with a friend.

    Estimate who is **heavier**: you or your friend.
    Now weigh each other. Write down your weights.
    Who is **heavier**? How much **heavier**?
    Do the same with other friends.

Livewire: Measures to level 3

Estimating weights

On this page you will learn how to estimate weights

BUZZWORD

Do you remember what **estimate** means? (page 8)

You will need kitchen scales or a balance and weights.

Choose the most sensible **estimate** of weight for each of these:

1 300 g   1 kg   3 kg

2 400 g   1 kg

3 300 g   900 g

4 300 g   3 kg

5 200 g   800 g

6 200 g   1 kg

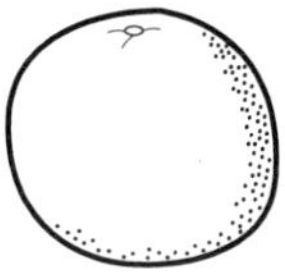

7 500 g   1 kg

8 100 g   1 kg

9 6 kg   1 kg

CHALLENGE!

I estimate 1 kg 200 grams.

I estimate 900 grams.

Play this game with a friend.

Take turns to choose an object to weigh.
Each player **estimates** its weight to the nearest 100 grams.
Weigh the object.
The player with the best **estimate** gets a point.
The first with 5 points wins the game.

Livewire: Measures to level 3

Glossary of buzzwords

approximately   **approximately** means about the same as

capacity   the **capacity** of something is how much it holds

contains   **contains** means has in it or holds

distance   **distance** is another word for length

estimate   **estimate** means make a careful guess

heavy, heavier, heaviest

height   **height** is how high or tall

length   **length** is how long

light, lighter, lightest

longer (in time)   is **longer** means takes more time

shorter (in time)   is **shorter** means takes less time.

via   **via** means going through

width   **width** is how wide